Pearson Canada

Supplemental Cases in Marketing

2006 Edition

Pearson Canada

Supplemental Cases in Marketing

2006 Edition

Cindy Stewart
Sauder School of Business
University of British Columbia

Toronto

Library and Archives Canada Cataloguing in Publication

Stewart, Cindy
Pearson Canada Supplemental Cases in Marketing / Cindy Stewart—2006 ed.

ISBN 0-13-198130-7

1. Winter Olympic Games (21st : 2010 : Vancouver, B.C.)—Economic aspects.

2. Sports—British Columbia—Vancouver—Marketing—Textbooks. I. Title.

GV842.2010.S84 2006   796.98'068'8   C2005-906698-9

ISBN 0-13-198130-7

Vice President, Editorial Director: Michael J. Young
Acquisitions Editor: Laura Forbes
Marketing Manager: Eileen Lasswell
Developmental Editor: Eleanor MacKay
Production Editor: Jen Handel
Copy Editor: Gilda Mekler
Production Coordinator: Andrea Falkenberg
Art Director: Julia Hall
Cover Design: Anthony Leung
Cover Image: Sports and Recreation/PhotoDisc

1 2 3 4 5   10 09 08 07 06

Printed and bound in the United States of America.

This book is dedicated to all colon cancer survivors pursuing their dream to live.

Contents

Topic Correlation Guide

This guide matches the marketing issues cases to introductory marketing topics.

Marketing Topics	Case(s)
Brand identity	1,2,4
Consumer research	4,8
e-marketing	3,8
Market segmentation	2,7,8
Marketing communications	2,3,4,8
Marketing ethics	1,3
New product development	6,7
Product pricing	4
Strategy	4,5,6,7

Preface

For many students new to marketing, learning the vocabulary for the breadth of concepts found in an introductory marketing textbook is demanding enough. Mastery of the concepts requires a well developed multidimensional perspective reflecting regional, national, and international competition; the type of good being marketed; the size of the firm in terms of financial, capital and human resources; and the maturity of the firm, the product, and the industry.

The faculty members in the Marketing Division at the Sauder School of Business have designed this booklet to help students begin developing perspective from examining the exciting and demanding challenges being faced by the many companies creating marketing strategies to achieve commercial Olympic dreams during the Vancouver–Whistler 2010 Winter Olympic Games. We'll explore the different perspectives of producing and marketing the Games for a range of companies from multinational corporations to SMEs in the profit and non-profit sectors.

Many Olympic dream decisions are being made today, while other companies haven't begun to consider how they might participate. For those companies planning today, much can change between now and February 2010. To capture the dynamic process of management decision making, the progress of each company will be tracked from now to 2010. Their progress and the major challenges faced along the way will be periodically reported in three planned updates. Case studies featuring new firms may also be added as the start date nears and more companies begin planning their Olympic dreams.

Since many students may be new to case-study-based learning, an abbreviated case-study format will be used to demonstrate textbook concepts in real business settings. Each case study will be followed by a set of questions to facilitate classroom discussion. To encourage students to learn more about each company and its Olympic aspirations, Internet references have been provided at the end of each case study, along with a glossary of new terms.

Marketing is an exciting, rigorous field of study that offers wonderfully diverse career paths ranging from highly quantitative consumer research to highly creative brand management, with something for everyone in between. The dynamic nature of consumer tastes and preferences requires a commitment to lifelong learning and guarantees you'll never become a victim of routine. We welcome you to the field of marketing and challenge you to participate in the creation of tomorrow's marketing knowledge.

Acknowledgments

To complete a project like this requires team work. I would like to take this time to express my sincerest gratitude to my team members:

To John Claxton (Sauder Business School), whose contribution, good counsel, and unwavering support of my academic indulgences made this booklet possible.

To Dale Griffin (Sauder Business School) for championing this project.

To Charles Weinberg and all the Marketing Division team members at the Sauder School of Business for their encouragement and contributions to this project.

To the many people at the various companies who have taken time from their busy schedules to share their stories.

To the many students I've had the privilege of teaching. Their enthusiastic pursuit of relevance to their world challenges me to grow as an educator and professional marketer.

Finally to my home team for their wisdom "to believe."

Part 1: Marketing Communications

1. Olympia Pizza

Creating and Protecting Your Brand

Remove them, we own them.

Cindy Stewart

A rose by any other name would smell as sweet—so the saying goes. Not so, says Mosi, owner of Olympia Pizza in Vancouver, British Columbia. Claiming an infringement of **trademark rights**, the Vancouver Olympic Corporation (Vanoc) ordered Olympia Pizza to cease and desist using the word "Olympia," the flame-bearing torch, and the multicoloured interlocking rings in his restaurant name and logo. Shortly thereafter, Vanoc amended their position to prohibit all new company names while grandfathering all existing company names having an Olympic reference—but the torch and rings still had to go.

Government-sponsored Olympic Games are a thing of the past. Today funding is provided by corporate sponsorship and licensing agreements. In exchange for their sizeable contribution to the Games, sponsoring companies are provided use of all Olympic imagery, the ability to display Olympic designations on products, and a number of other benefits[1]. To protect the investment of

---

[1] Other exclusive benefits include hospitality opportunities at the Olympic Games; direct advertising and promotional opportunities (including preferential access to Olympic broadcast advertising); on-site concessions/franchise and product sale/showcase opportunities; ambush marketing protection; and acknowledgement of their support though a broad Olympic sponsorship recognition program.

their sponsors and licensees, Vanoc must prevent the Olympic brand assets from attaining "free good" status by preventing all unauthorized use of the brand assets. The most recognized of these assets are the name, the five multi-coloured interlocking rings, and the flaming burning torch. All the Olympic assets are listed on Vanoc's official web site,[2] which clearly states that authorization is required.

History of Olympia Pizza

Olympia Pizza exterior

Traditional symbols such as the pillars of the Palaestra, flame-bearing torches, and colourful intertwined rings became part of the company logo, and these symbols adorned the windows, menus, and exterior signage. An authentic, Greek branded dining experience was created by the restaurant's colour palette of azure blue and white (the national colours of Greece), hand-painted wall frescoes, home-style Mediterranean menu offerings (including the national treasure, baklava), traditional Greek music, and a typography reminiscent of the Greek alphabet.

Mosi began working as a cook at Olympia Pizza in 1990 and bought the restaurant two years later. Since then little has changed at Olympia Pizza. Even the staff have remained the same, the newest employee being a four-year veteran. In 1998 the restaurant interior was modernized and the menus were updated, mostly to celebrate community accolades, including Best Take Out 2001, Best Baklava, and Best Pizza Crust. The consistent food quality, hospitality, and value keep local residents coming back for more: 90% of the restaurant's annual revenue is generated by the weekly visits of local residents.

Creating Unique Value

All companies selling a product or service create brands. Over time these brands often develop into the firm's most valued assets.[3] Brand development has evolved from creating a name, a logo, and a tagline into the formation of a multidimensional, interactive brand identity. Today a brand is more often

---

[2] A listing of names and artworks owned by the International Organising Committee (IOC) and Vanoc are listed in the Brand and Logo Guidelines published by Vanoc. See www.vancouver2010.com/Emblem/protection.htm.

[3] To view Interbrand's annual list of The 100 Best Global Brands By Value, visit www.interbrand.com.

underpinned by how it identifies with the consumer on a personal level rather than by the functional benefits it provides the user.

In addition to a name, logo, and tagline creating a brand today includes a **corporate identity**, value proposition, and personality. When selecting a name, companies choose between function-oriented names such as Olympia Pizza™ or Windex™ and abstract names like Nokia™ or Tylenol™. A function-oriented name references the functional benefits a consumer will receive when using the product. For an abstract brand name, the functional benefits received from using the product are learned by association. Developing associations requires repeated exposure to a marketing message. This makes abstract brand names more expensive to create; however, a more complex meaning and longer memory recall often result.

A product's value consists of both the actual and perceived functional and emotional benefits that the brand promises to deliver to all its constituents. This promise is defined by the brand's **value proposition** and corporate identity. Brand consumers and stakeholders connect with these benefits on a variety of levels: the satisfaction or pleasure from the utility received; the sense of belonging or status conferred; or as a friend. However, promises are not enough; the customer must view the company's offering as a real and unique value, and the company must be able to consistently deliver a clear, compelling brand experience.

What makes a meal at Olympia Pizza unique and compelling? Perhaps it is the way staff greet regular guests by first name and stop to chat, or the restaurant's patio, award-winning food, and reasonable prices, the Greek décor, the Christmas dinner appreciation program...the experience is more than the sum of these parts. Olympia Pizza promises to consistently deliver a familiar Greek-style dinner created from family recipes, offering something for everybody at a price that makes dining in Mosi's kitchen with friends a much better alternative to eating alone in yours.

Understanding how customers evaluate their consumption experience and then using this information to consistently deliver the brand promise to exceed expectations has catapulted Olympia Pizza to "classic" status in the highly competitive, fashionable Vancouver restaurant scene. Now that's real brand equity.

Finding A Resolution

In keeping with his generous demeanour, Mosi first offered to cover up the signage. Then he offered to close the restaurant for the 17 days of the Games to ensure that no visitor mistakes Olympia Pizza for an official "Olympic" restaurant. But he won't consider changing the signage because of the signal it would send to the surrounding community. Every year 10 new signs go up on Denman Street, with the closure of 10 businesses that didn't make it. If Olympia Pizza were to change its signage, the neighbourhood residents would instantly conclude that the restaurant is under new ownership and many customers would not return.

Furthermore, Mosi believes that the disputed symbols are in the **public domain**. So do some 4000 petition signers and a high-profile trademark lawyer (willing to champion his cause pro bono). But even if the protected name and symbols

Olympia Pizza exterior signage

are not in the public domain, the trademark holder must take swift action to enforce their exclusive rights; simply registering the trademark is not enough. "It's very simple—I'm right," says Mosi.

Questions for Discussion

1. Do you agree that the name Olympia, the flame-bearing torch, and the multi-coloured interlocking rings are in the public domain? How do you know?

2. What do you feel is the best solution for this issue?

3. What could the original owner of Olympia Pizza have done to avoid the problems experienced by Mosi today?

Glossary

Trademark Rights—statute law prohibiting the unauthorized use of names, taglines, and artworks by companies and persons other than the registered trademark holder.

Corporate Identity—includes the vision, mission, and value statements of a company.

Value Proposition—includes the all the functional and emotional benefits received by a consumer from the use of a product.

Public Domain—free availability of a name or other item of intellectual property; when the public uses the protected name of a product as a common noun, it is said to have become a generic term and has lost its exclusive rights.

Web Links

www.998denman.com is the website for Olympia Pizza.

www.olympic.org is the website for the International Olympic Committee.

www.vancouver2010.com is the website for The Vancouver Olympic Committee.

The Government of Canada website **www.strategis.ic.gc.ca/sc_mrksv/cipo** provides information on registering and searching trademarks and other intellectual property.

The Government of Canada website **http://laws.justice.gc.ca/en/t-13/106520.html** provides a digital version of the *Trade-marks Act (R.S. 1985, c. T-13)*.

2. McDonald's Inc.

Developing Integrated Marketing Communication Plans

The world's best grill team serving Olympians

Cindy Stewart

After successfully meeting the needs of children and moms around the world for 20 years, McDonald's was served a wake-up call in 2002: the first reported loss in 30 years, falling share price, and a decline in brand relevancy. When looking back to determine what had gone wrong, Larry Light, Chief Global Marketing Officer at McDonald's, quickly concluded that McDonald's was overly supply-focused. People ate at McDonald's because it was cheap and convenient. Furthermore, the solution wasn't to find new customers, stated Christine Davies, Director of Communications for McDonald's Canada. Just like some parents, McDonald's had lost touch with its kid customers as they matured into 40.5 million teenagers and young adults with a love for fast food and a burgeoning collective wallet of $420 million dollars[1].

McDonald's recent marketing strategy is really about "brand journalism": telling different stories to several demographic groups through a variety of media, while ensuring that all those communications reinforce a single brand image. McDonald's set out to reconnect in a fresh and relevant way with the alienated young adults aged 15 to 24. Starting with their passion points of music, sports, fashion, and entertainment,[2] marketing campaigns were redefined to capture the imagination of youth yet reflect the brand's family values heritage.

In September of 2003, the "i'm lovin' it" **promotional campaign** was launched in Munich, Germany,[3] with overwhelming success: 89% brand awareness among young

---

[1] "The US Youth Market", *Packaged Facts,* July 2003, available at www.marketresearch.com.

[2] Wayne Chmiel, McDonald's Director of Marketing Worldwide, International Business Conference, Sauder Business School, Vancouver, March 4, 2005.

[3] The U.S. campaign is a multi-agency effort, featuring five adult-focused commercials created by Heye & Partner, part of the worldwide DDB network and a long-time McDonald's agency based in Uterhaching, Germany. Source: www.mcdonalds.com.

adults, *Advertising Age* Marketer of the Year 2004 award, and a 25% increase in global restaurant sales. Reflecting a passion for music, McDonald's partnered with pop culture icons such as Justin Timberlake, Destiny's Child, and international stars Leehom Wang and Alejandro Fernandez. Promoting the healthy choices and active lifestyle values of the brand, ties to sporting activities were strengthened by adding Yao Ming to its star roster and broadening event sponsorships to include skateboarder Tony Hawk. Other marketing changes include the sponsorship of an MTV program showcasing new musical talent; additions to the healthier choices menu; and gaming and text messaging promotions in the United States. Even the world's favourite clown, Ronald McDonald, has undergone a makeover.

What hasn't changed is McDonald's sponsorship of the Olympic Games. Since the hamburger airlift of 1968 to Grenoble, France, McDonald's has been serving its famous menu to Olympic athletes, coaches, and spectators from around the world at its namesake restaurants in the heart of the Olympic Village, at the Main Media Center, in Olympic Park, and in its restaurants throughout the respective host cities[4]. McDonald's first became an Official Sponsor of the 1976 Olympic Games in Montreal. In 1996, McDonald's extended its

long-standing commitment to the Olympic Movement by joining the Top Olympic Program (TOP) and becoming a Worldwide Sponsor, providing the support needed for staging the Olympic Games, for National Olympic Committees, for athletes and teams, and for the entire Olympic Movement. By the 2012 Summer Games, McDonald's will have been a TOP Games Sponsor for twelve consecutive years. McDonald's will spend an estimated $80 million for its 2008–2012 TOP membership[5]. This amount does not reflect the millions of additional dollars spent on ads aired on the official television networks at an estimated cost of $730 000 per 30-second prime time ad,[6] nor the millions of dollars spent on Olympic activation events held around the world[7].

---

[4] During the 2004 Summer Games more than 300 000 athletes, coaches, officials and spectators were served around the clock for 33 days—an estimated 230 000 Big Macs, 40 000 servings of World-famous fries, 100 000 Premium salads, and 220 000 orders of Chicken McNuggets—or 2 000 000 meat patties, 414 469 pounds of potatoes and 26 455 pounds of lettuce.

[5] "Brand Strategy Briefing: Olympic fees for mega events," *Brand Strategy,* 15 September 2004.

[6] "Athens Battle Ghost of Sydney," August 2004, available at http://money.cnn.com.

[7] During the 1996 Games McDonald's was estimated to have spent over $300 million on television ads and on-site promotions related to Olympic sponsorship (Miyazaki, Morgan, *Journal of Advertising Research,* January 2001).

McDonald's participation in the TOP sponsorship program is bigger than connecting with young adults on their passion point of sport, says Light. It creates an opportunity to simultaneously address all McDonald's brand fans with marketing designed to connect the brand with people's lives, based on shared attitudes and values. Many of the Olympic activation events are **grassroots marketing programs** designed to keep all family members connected with the brand. The Olympic Day Run, held worldwide in 150 countries, is an all ages "fun run" promoting Olympic ideals and a healthy active lifestyle. McDonald's Canada

recently launched its GO Active!™ Olympic Fitness Challenge, in which participating elementary grade students are rewarded for improvements in fitness during the school year[8]. Perhaps the Olympic themed event dearest to the hearts of McDonald's employees is the Olympic Champion Crew program.

More than 1.5 million McDonald's employees from more than 100 countries compete for the opportunity to become a member of McDonald's Olympic Champion Crew. Like the path of an Olympic athlete, the road to becoming a Crew Olympian requires training and commitment. Each participant works his or her way through local, regional and then national championships[9]. The selection process is determined by each country, based on criteria of excellence in teamwork, speed, accuracy, and "i'm lovin' it" service.

At the end of the day, even the losers are winners; McDonald's acknowledges the hard work of all national participants by rewarding and recognizing them just for competing.[10] International Olympic Champion Crew members get the chance to experience the Olympics firsthand with a paid trip to the Olympic Games. As a member of the McDonald's Olympic Champion Crew, employees have the opportunity to serve the world's best athletes at the Olympic Games. In addition, they enjoy attending Olympic events, participating in special recreational and cultural activities, and even have the opportunity to showcase their talents in the Big Mac Build Event—a race against the clock by Champion Olympic Crew members and teams of Olympic athletes and celebrities to build the most Big Macs™.

---

[8] "McDonald's and the COC launch the Go Active!™ Olympic Fitness Challenge," *Canada Newswire*, 22 September 2004

[9] "McDonalds Kicks Off All-American Crew Competition," September 2001, available at www.foodservices.com.

[10] Ben Van Houten, "Game Plan," *Restaurant Business*, June 2001, p. 42.

The Olympic Champion Crew program relates to employee development, motivation, and retention. According to Davies, the majority of McDonald's employees and management start as restaurant crew and grow within the company to reach their personal goals. This internal employee development program is designed to reinforce McDonald's company values and Olympic ideals. Working at McDonald's is not just a McJob, stated Davies, it's about promotion of the self and your skills.

During the Olympic Games in Athens, more than 3.6 billion people worldwide watched on TV.[11] Although televised coverage of the Olympic Games consistently dominates its time slot, only 16.3% of these viewers were young adults.[12] World Cup Soccer attracts a more youthful audience than the Olympics.[13] Young adults are more interested in surfing, snowboarding, skateboarding, BMX biking, and motocross[14] than in most of the 28 sports featured during the Olympic Games. Even though McDonald's achieved the second-best Olympic advertising results for a non-sporting goods company, according to the Chartered Institute of Marketing (CIM) only 15% of **respondents** correctly identified McDonald's as an official sponsor of the Sydney Olympic Games.

According to TNS Media Intelligence/CMR data covering July 2003 through May 2004, McDonald's spent $572.8 million on measured-media advertising and an estimated $754 million in 2004 on promotions, direct marketing, and public relations (according to *PROMO* magazine), for an estimated annual global marketing budget of $1.2 billion to appeal to everyone who is young at heart. Whether it was the Athens Olympic Games or the "i'm lovin' it" ads, something was working in 2004 for McDonald's. Global sales were up 6.9%; there were positive same-store sales in every month, which hadn't happened for 17 years; and U.S. restaurant sales were up 9.6%—the highest annual result in 30 years.[15] It looks like as though young adults' attention has certainly been grabbed, but keeping these fast-food-friendly consumers in the restaurant once the next new thing comes along might be a far greater challenge.

---

[11] "Athens Olympics Draw Record TV Audience," October 2004, available at www.wjla.com.

[12] "Sports Marketing: Going for Gold – Olympics coverage marketing," *American Demographics,* July 2000.

[13] Rana Dogar, "Too Much Is About Right," *Newsweek,* June 15, 1998, p. 35.

[14] "The US Youth Market," *Packaged Facts,* July, 2003, available at www.marketresearch.com.

[15] "Thoroughly Modern Marketing: McDonalds's updates advertising to remain 'forever young,'" *Nation's Restaurant News,* April, 2005.

Questions For Discussion

1. How large an impact does the "i'm lovin' it" theme have on a young adult's decision about fast-food restaurant selection? What do you think has the biggest influence?

2. How important do you feel the Olympic Champion Crew is to developing the motivation of McDonald's employees? Could the same results be achieved using different events?

3. Do you think McDonald's should continue their TOP Sponsorship support of the Olympics? Are there other events that could achieve the same results more economically?

4. Is there another segment of the fast-food market McDonald's should be making its primary marketing target?

Glossary

Promotional Campaign—a coordinated series of promotional efforts built around a single theme and designed to achieve a specific objective.

Grassroots Marketing Programs—programs that seek to connect with existing and prospective customers using non-mainstream media methods focused on building strong client relationships with the brand.

Respondents—individual participants in a marketing research project.

Web Links

www.goactive.ca is the website operated by McDonald's Canada in support of its Olympic Fitness program targeted to elementary school students.

www.mcdonalds.ca is the website for McDonald's Canada.

www.advertsingage.com is the website for *Advertising Age* magazine.

3. Wasatch Brewery Company

Sporting Event Sponsorship

When playing by the rules, be creative.

Cindy Stewart

Growing up in the shadows of the Miller Brewing Company did not inspire Greg Schirf's passion for brew. He truly discovered beer during a family trek to Germany when he was 17 years old—and it didn't taste like anything at home. Schirf's discerning taste would be further refined during his years of study in Rome. After returning home to Milwaukee to complete his philosophy degree at Marquette University, Schirf turned his pining for European-style beer into producing specialty beer. Although he didn't profit much then, the demand from friends always outpaced the supply.

History of Wasatch Beer

Once school was out, Schirf headed west to Park City, Utah, with his brother, to become land barons. After 10 years of riding the real estate boom-and-bust cycles, Schirf was done. His next move resulted from a chance meeting in Seattle in 1985 with his beer hero, Tom Baune of Pyramid Beer. With the encouragement of their developing friendship. he started the Schirf Brewing Company. Being located in a state where religious traditions had led to restrictive alcohol laws didn't deter Schirf; his family had a history of successful prohibition entrepreneurship. Instead Schirf quickly concluded Utah must be teeming with parched beer lovers. It had been two decades since the residents of the state had had a legal local brewery.

In 1986 Schirf began serving his award winning[1] European-style beers at his beer-only establishment,[2] Wasatch Brewery—Utah's first microbrewery. Not surprisingly, it

---

[1] Gold medal winner at World Beer Cup 2004. Winners were selected by an international panel of 93 beer judges from an impressive field of 1594 entries received from 392 breweries in 40 countries. More than 3800 breweries in 100 countries were invited to compete.

[2] Utah laws limit primary alcohol in cocktails to one ounce, one drink at a time. Beer must have an alcohol content no greater than 3.2%, and must be served at beer-only establishments. Anything more is available only at government-controlled liquor stores andprivate clubs, which require a membership fee of $5 a day or $18 per year.

quickly became one of the most popular spots in Park City. Soon demand outpaced the brewery's capacity, so Schirf launched a successful challenge to state alcohol laws for the construction of a 15-barrel-capacity brew pub. The Wasatch family of beer also hit the road to 10 states, including Illinois, Idaho, California and Washington. To meet the increased sales, additional production facilities would be required. Planning the construction of a new, top-of-the-line 50-barrel microbrewery in Salt Lake City was slow. All the while competition rapidly intensified, as many other micro- and macro-breweries started jumping on the craft brewery bandwagon. Wasatch brands were feeling the heat in other states too. Established brands such as Sam Adams™ and Red Hook™ had well-established **distribution networks** that were making it tough for Wasatch beers to get on tap.

From the day the Salt Lake Brewery finally opened, it was plagued with excess capacity. "The business plan needed to be revisited," says Schirf, "and we decided to concentrate on owning our backyard." All the brands were pulled back to Utah. Another local microbrewery, Squatters, was approached to share the Salt Lake plant facilities. However, production scheduling became a problem, causing the co-op partner to become a merger target. All ten brands survived the merger and continued to be sold under their original brand banners.

Olympic Ambush

About the same time, the Olympics were coming to town. During the bid process the Utah Bid Committee often called on the Wasatch Brewery to provided beer and in-kind support for events surrounding IOC member visits. But when it came time for contracts to be assigned, Schirf quickly learned that when it comes to the Olympics, local support is no match for the goliath-sized sponsorship partners. Schirf had a sponsorship budget of about US$5000 US; Budweiser paid US$50 000 000 to be the "official" alcoholic beverage sponsor to the Utah Games.

Feeling slighted, Schirf decided to take on his deep-pocket rivals and the State of Utah. He waited until the countdown to the Games began before launching a series of billboard and radio media blitzes designed to poke fun at the inequities. The first State attack was the introduction of Polygamy Porter brand beer and its taglines, "Why Stop At One?" and "Take Some Home for the Wives." Leveraging the young brides of Polygamy Porter, the stunningly attractive St. Provo Girl[3] missionary with "nice cans"

---

[3] Alise Ingrid Liepnieks, a native Utahn and former U.S. snowboard team member whose career was cut short due to a back injury suffered during a snowboard competition in 1993. Unaware of the severity of the injury, she competed in a half-pipe exhibition and lost feeling in both her legs.

was next introduced, encouraging residents to join "the other religion" and "baptize their taste buds" with Squatter's brand beer.

Concurrent Olympic campaigns included "Unofficial Beer of the Winter Games" and "Unofficial Amber Ale ~~2002~~" assaults. Once the Games arrived, every day the Wasatch keg sled pulled by yellow labs followed behind the Budweiser Clydesdales wagon in the Parade of Champions. While Bud was being served up in the "official" beer gardens, so too was Wasatch beer a stone's throw away on Salt Lake City property. The most powerful weapon of all proved to be Provo Girl; she was set loose on the crowds like a modern-day Pied Piper to lead them into the Wasatch beer tent.

Claiming Victory

"Ultimately, I was the victim of my own success," exclaims Schirf. First the largest billboard company refused to run the Polygamy Porter ads. However, the smaller, starving companies were eagerly waiting in the wings for the business. Next the State tried to outlaw religious references in alcohol advertising, but they were forced to back down with egg on their face.[4] Then the Salt Lake City Olympic Organizing Committee (SLOC) sent a **cease-and-desist order** demanding the use of "Winter Games" be stopped, followed by a claim they owned the "2002" in "Unofficial Amber Ale." But the epitome of success, according to Schirf, was a threatened lawsuit from St. Pauli Beer of Germany over St. Provo Girl. To make these people go away, the saint was dropped to rename her Provo Girl.[5] The problems with SLOC miraculously disappeared when the bribery scandal inspired a campaign of T-shirts reading "Beer not Bribery."

To capitalize on the **buzz**, Wasatch Brewery became one of the most successful T-shirt vendors at the Olympic Games. Liquor laws in the state of Utah prohibit the sale of cased beer from the brewery directly to the consumer. Total T-shirt sales revenue was about US$2000 in a typical month. As a result of the Polygamy Porter campaign, T-shirt sales skyrocketed to US$55 000 in one month, and total T-shirt sales accounted for approximately 20% of revenue generated from the Olympics. Today, the list of branded products offered on the company website has expanded to include headwear, glassware (pint, shot, and pilsner glasses, beer mugs, coffee mugs, and travel mugs); clothing (T-shirts, sweatshirts, collared shirts, bike shirts, and vests); miscellaneous

---

[4] The Utah Department of Alcohol Beverage Control (UDABC) attempted to revise its rules as a result of a federal court constitutional challenge. The draft "new rules" included a prohibition of religious-themed advertising that would have prohibited Wasatch advertising as well as all kosher, sacramental or Christian-themed products. Not intending the latter outcome, UDABC dropped the anti-religion clause in the legislation.

[5] In response a new Provo Girl campaign was launched: "I may be from Provo but I Ain't No Saint".

(playing cards, bottle coolers, and tavern signs); and commemorative pins. Sales of these products account for 5% of total annual revenue.

The diffusion of buzz was phenomenal. T-shirt sales from the company website followed the location of current media coverage. At first orders were just in North America and then they fanned out to faraway places such as Japan, Russia, and Africa. Line-ups at the beer tents signalled local media success: the Wasatch beer tent line-up was typically three times as long as Budweiser's.

Since cross-state-border sales weren't an option, Schirf's Olympic investment payoff was completely dependent on post-Games tourism generated by State tourism marketing campaigns. Olympic memories fade fast after the close of the Games. Hosting cities must keep the legacy active in the public consciousness if they want to capitalize on their investment. A State budget shortfall, pending war, and economic uncertainty all meant that Utah never experienced the post-Olympic surge in international tourism it had expected. In 2002 domestic leisure travel from western states was the only source of tourism growth for state tourism.[6] While it is hard to measure, Schirf estimates website product sales relating to the Olympics were US$150,000 in 2002 and trailed off to around US $50 000 in 2003 and 2004.

Sage from the Heart

Recently Schirf was asked what advice he had for Vancouver companies wanting to cash in on the 2010 Olympic Games. He suggested that companies should identify their true possibilities for international sales. If they don't exist, then the company should concentrate on developing **a local market brand identity**—visitors will love it. Accept the fact that you will never make "official" status and find creative ways to reach "unofficial" status in the public's hearts and minds. Push boundaries but know when to back off. Once the media event has occurred, settle any arising disputes out of court, because you've already won the exposure battle.

---

[6] "Utah's Olympic Legacy: promotion of the Olympic experience focused on the West", *TravelAge West*, February 24, 2003.

Questions For Discussion

1. When Wasatch and Squatter's merged, should any of the beer brands in either company been killed off?

2. Do you feel the religious themes and ambush marketing tactics used by Wasatch Brewery are ethical?

3. During the Olympic Games, what was the primary business of Wasatch Brewery?

4. What other post-Olympic business strategies could Wasatch Brewery have pursued?

Glossary

Distribution Networks—organized systems of formal or informal relationships between companies which, in combination, move the product from the manufacturing floor to the end customers for purchase.

Buzz—a flurry of word-of-mouth exchanges between consumers resulting from a unique and memorable communication strategy or special event designed to create publicity for a product or firm.

Local Market Brand Identity—a brand identity highlighting the company's roots in the country of origin.

Cease-and-Desist Order—a formal letter issued by legal counsel requesting that the recipient immediately stop an activity that is alleged to violate the issuer's legal rights.

Web Links

www.wasatchbeers.com is the "official" website for Wasatch Brewing Company.

www.squatters.com is the "official" website for the Squatters family of beers, including Provo Girl Pilsner.

www.beertown.org is the website for the World Beer Cup Competition.

Part 2: Marketing Strategies

4. *Hollywood Rebel Studios*

Advertising at the Olympics[1]

Tirtha Dhar, Jason Ho, and Charles B. Weinberg

Aidan J. Remy, president of Hollywood Rebel Studio (HRS), had to decide whether to submit a bid to have his movie studio be the exclusive primetime broadcast TV advertiser of movies at the 2010 Winter Olympics. This was a complicated decision for several reasons. First, he had to make this decision several years in advance and without knowing what movies he would have on the market in 2010. Second, this would involve a commitment of at least $27.5 million. And third, the cost per thousand viewers would be approximately twice the amount that would be charged for television network advertising on regular shows.

The marketing director of HRS, Samuel Paul, was strongly urging this commitment. Samuel argued that HRS, as well as several other major movie companies, had for years been using big-event advertising to

---

[1] Copyright © 2005 Charles B. Weinberg

promote their movies.[2] In 2005, for example, eight movies such as *The Pacifier* had each spent $2.4 million for a 30-second spot on the U.S. national broadcast of the Super Bowl. One recent study had suggested that Super Bowl ads cost three times as much per thousand viewers (CPM) as advertising on regular network shows. Moreover, Samuel suggested that not only would the Olympics provide an unprecedented opportunity to launch HRS' movies, but it would deny its competitors an opportunity to do so. With the 2010 Winter Olympics occurring in February, this would be a great time to begin the marketing of summer blockbusters, which actually start showing in May. (Two such blockbusters were launched in 2005: *Star Wars III: Revenge of the Sith* and *Madagascar*.)

On the other hand, the financial director, Joshua M. Atthew, was quite cautious about committing such a large sum of money. Although he noted that, in 2002, the average movie had a production budget of $59 million and an advertising budget of $27 million (approximately $11 million for television advertising), he also pointed out that the average movie had a North American box office of $33 million. Most movies had to depend on overseas markets and DVD sales if they were to cover their production costs.

The North American Movie Industry

The movie industry is not only glamorous, but is also economically significant. It is the US's largest export industry. According to data from the 2002 MPAA Economic Report (www.mpaa.org), the domestic box office totaled $9.5 billion, and the international box office gross was $9.6 billion, but the VHS and DVD rental and sales market totaled more than $20 billion.[3] Each year, the eight major movie studios (such as Warner Brothers, Fox, Universal, and Disney) release 200–250 movies. A studio such as HRS might release 20–25 movies in the course of a year. Even for wide release movies, the range of movies is

---

[2] According to Geri Wang, senior vice president for prime-time sales at the ABC Television Network unit of ABC in New York, "Clients are using the Academy Awards and the Super Bowl, as a showcase vehicle to break new creative and launch new brands".

[3] For historical reasons, "domestic" box office revenue typically refers to revenues in both the United States and Canada.

enormous. At the high end would be a movie such as *Star Wars: Revenge of the Sith,* which in its first week generated box-office revenues of $200 million and cost an estimated $115 million to produce. At the low end among wide release movies (defined as those shown in at least 600 of the 37 000 theaters in the United States), might be a movie such as *Crash*, which opened in 1864 theaters and achieved a box-office revenue of $13 million in the first week. Overall, the movie audience is younger than that of the overall population. For example, people aged 16–29 make up only 24% of the U.S. population but account for 40% of box-office admissions. People over 50 years of age make up a third of the U.S. population, but represent only 17% of movie admissions. So a movie like *Ladies in Lavender*, which appealed to this segment and starred Judi Dench and Maggie Smith, stands in contrast to most wide releases, which appeal to a younger audience. After two weeks, *Lavender* was running in 54 theatres after two weeks with total box-office receipts of $395 000. Even within the younger audience, there are many segments.

Approximately 50% of a movie's box-office revenue is retained by the exhibitor (such as Loew's Cineplex Odeon or Famous Players). Many movies do not cover their costs, and for those that do, revenues from videotapes and DVDs are often critical to achieving that success. Nevertheless, many industry observers believe that achieving high box-office sales in the first weekend of a movie's release is critical. For the 139 wide-release movies in 2002, there was a correlation (r^2) of 0.94 between first-week box-office revenues and total box-office revenues. The correlation (r^2) between the sales of the top 50 DVDs in 2002 and the box-office revenues was 0.65. In contrast to many new products, the first week of a movie's box office was usually the best, with sales declining approximately exponentially over time.

Hollywood Rebel Studio

HRS (disguised name) is one of the major California-based movie studios. For a number of years, like most of the major studios, HRS had been owned by a large conglomerate. While the new owners had brought a more analytic approach to decision making, there were still many in the industry who believed that the most critical decisions were the artistic ones and relied heavily on intuition. Nevertheless, managers such as Joshua Atthew, who earned his MBA from the University of British Columbia, had shown the value of careful analysis in decision making.

In the last year, HRS had released 20 movies and had achieved average revenue of $45 million (somewhat above the industry average). Under the guidance of Sam Paul, HRS had adopted aggressive marketing strategies that focused on achieving high first-week box office sales. While the strategy would vary by movie, Sam Paul believed that wide distribution made movies easy for people to see, and he used intensive marketing to get people to the box office with heavy advertising. He believed that it was marketing's job to drive the first week's sales, and then audience reaction would determine how well the opening-week box office would hold up over subsequent weeks. Marketing strategy after the first week was designed to support the movie and build on (hopefully) good word-of-mouth.

HRS was trying to increase the impact of advertising. People often used their remote control to switch away when a commercial was showing. In addition, with the increasing availability of digital video recorders and decline in viewers of the national networks, advertisers were looking for new ways to break through the clutter. One approach was to use new methods of **viral marketing** (as occurred for the *Blair Witch Project*); another was to use **product placement**. For example, Ford was reported to have paid $35 million for the Ford-owned Aston Martin to be James Bond's car, replacing BMW in the 2002 sequel *Die Another Day*. Marketers have seen many product placement success stories over the years: In the 1967 classic film *The Graduate*, Dustin Hoffman drove an Alfa Romeo, and the Italian carmaker immediately felt the results in the form of improved sales. In 2004, Pepsi managed to get placed in seven blockbuster films. Computer maker Apple is especially active in the field; their computers have had bit parts in films from *Independence Day* to *Garfield*.

Other advertisers had sought to associate themselves with major events. For example, a company could become a title sponsor for a Professional Golf Association (PGA) tournament for a fee of $6 million in 2005. In addition, HRS wanted to find ways to stand out from other movies in a cluttered market. One way to stand out and obtain viewer attention was to advertise at major events. For example, in 2002, nine movies advertised on the Super Bowl, paying an estimated $2.2 million per 30-second ad.

The 2010 Olympics in Vancouver

On July 2, 2003, the International Olympic Committee (IOC) announced that Vancouver would be the host for the 2010 Olympics. Earlier in 2003, the IOC had awarded NBC the rights to broadcast exclusively the 2010 Winter Olympics and the 2012 Summer Olympics, with a bid of $2 billion for the TV and broadcast rights (including the Internet); in addition, GE, the parent company of NBC, became an official Olympics sponsor for an additional sum of nearly $200 million. In Canada, CTV became the exclusive broadcaster for the Winter Olympics by outbidding CBC for the first time in the history of Canadian Olympic broadcasting. HRS' main focus was on the U.S. market, but the company would likely attempt to replicate any arrangement it made with NBC with CTV as well.

The Winter Olympics has been a major television event in North America, and the 2002 Winter Olympic at Salt Lake City, Utah, was one of the most successful in North America. In the United States, over the 19 days of Olympic broadcasting, 187 million people tuned into the event, watching on average 29 hours. This also implies a total of 5.1 billion viewer hours of Winter Games action, watched by 75% of the U.S. population—more than double the viewing of the Nagano 1998 Winter Olympics. NBC prime-time ratings were higher every night of the Games than all their rivals combined, and the Opening Ceremony attracted a rating of 27.4, an all-time high for any Olympic Ceremony, winter or summer. The women's figure skating free program, with 68 million viewers, was the highest-rated prime-time Thursday program on any U.S. network television since 1998. Dick

Ebersol, Chairman of NBC Sports and Olympics, said, "These Games surpassed my wildest expectations. Far and away the best Games I have ever been involved in."

In Canada there were 691 hours of coverage; an all-time television viewing record of 8.6 million viewers for Canada was generated during the U.S. men's ice hockey final on CBC. Given that Vancouver 2010 will bring the games back to North America, broadcasters and advertisers were anticipating high ratings.

Just as NBC had committed far in advance for the Olympics, it was now providing advertisers an opportunity to buy advertising time far in advance. In particular, NBC was providing the opportunity for companies in different industries to be the lead prime-time advertiser through a bidding process. A prime-time exclusive slot means that the advertiser will have no competitors in its field advertising during prime time broadcasting. This bidding process will be in two phases, starting from 2007 to 2008. It is generally assumed that all the prime-time slots will be sold out in the 2007 round of bidding. While no price had yet been discussed, Aidan Remy felt that a minimum bid of $25 million would be required. He also estimated that the cost per thousand viewers (CPM) would probably be about twice the CPM for regular network advertising. In Canada, a similar bidding process would be initiated by CTV, with an expected price of approximately $2.5 million.

While respecting the views of Sam and Joshua, Aidan asked if there been an economic analysis of such advertising. While there had been no such study for the Olympics, Joshua had found a study on the web that examined the effectiveness of Super Bowl advertising. Fortunately for HRS, the study had used movies as the test industry and attempted to examine the effect of Super Bowl advertising as compared to regular advertising on the number of theatres showing the movie and the first week's box office.

The Super Bowl Study

Researchers had conducted a study of all the movies advertised in the 2000–2002 Super Bowl. Nineteen movies were advertised on the

Super Bowl in those three years. The movies came from a range of genres and MPAA rating categories (R, PG-13, PG, and G) and were not exclusively big-budget movies. While only four of the movies were to be released within a month of the Super Bowl, the advertised movies were all to be released within six months of the Super Bowl. For all but four of the movies, the Super Bowl was the first major television advertising expenditure. For comparison purposes, the analysts had gathered data on all the other wide-release movies. The Super Bowl movies tended to have larger production budgets and higher advertising budgets. Movies advertised on the Super Bowl were also less likely to be rated G than the other movies.

To control for the impact of other variables, the research team had conducted a nonlinear, **multivariate regression analysis**. While there were a number of interesting findings, the HRS executives were primarily interested in two results. First, the analysis showed that advertising can have both a direct and indirect effect on first-week box-office sales. Advertising affects the number of theatres showing a movie—the higher the advertising, the more theatres show a movie, even after controlling for such other factors as production budget. In turn, the more theatres show the movie, the higher the first week attendance.

Second, both Super Bowl and other advertising have an overall positive effect on sales. In one simulation analysis, the researchers asked what would be the effect of spending an additional $2.2 million on either a Super Bowl ad or on regular television advertising. A typical movie in the sample spent $12 million on television advertising prior to the launch of a movie, but did not spend any money on the Super Bowl. Such a movie would be expected to generate an extra $4.3 million in first-week box office if it spent an additional $2.2 million on regular television advertising However, if the same sum were spent on Super Bowl advertising, it would generate an extra $12.7 million in first-week box office. On the other hand, if a movie that already advertised on the Super Bowl spent an additional $2.2 million for a second Super Bowl spot, its first-week box office revenues would be expected to increase by only $1.1 million. Of course, if too many movies advertised during the Super Bowl, results might be diminished.

The Decision

Sam felt the Super Bowl results strengthened his argument. If advertising for one day in February could increase box-office revenues, imagine what 19 days of exclusive prime-time movie advertising could do! Just like the Super Bowl, the Olympics are a live event that people want to see. They pay attention to this type of event, both because they enjoy it and because they want to be able to talk about it the next day with their friends. Joshua was not so convinced. He pointed out that even if the first Super Bowl ad was effective, the second one might not be. The Olympic ads will air many times. And, of course, the average ratings of the Olympics are much below those of the Super Bowl, so the coverage is not as wide. Although in recent years Super Bowl viewership has been stagnant, according to Nielsen Media Research, in 2005 The New England Patriots' Super Bowl victory over the Philadelphia Eagles was seen by an estimated 86.1 million people, down 4% from a Nielsen rating of 44.2 in 2004. (A ratings point represents 1 096 000 households, or 1% of the nation's estimated 109.6 million TV homes.)

Aidan reminded his executives that they had to make a decision soon. They had to decide not only whether to bid, but how much. While NBC paid $400 million more than the next bid—$1.8 billion from Disney-owned ABC—CBS did not bid and Fox bid $1.3 billion. Of course, NBC had made an estimated profit of $100 million on the 2002 Salt Lake City Olympics. On the other hand, other studios might be planning similar strategies. NBC's recent takeover of Universal Studios from Vivendi might also complicate the process of negotiation. But as part of the contract with IOC, Universal would have to negotiate independently with NBC, just like any other advertiser.

Aidan felt that this was going to be a tough decision. Advertising during the Olympics would imply diverting advertising expenses from traditional and other big-event media advertising—and there are other opportunities for sponsors. For example, the February 2005 calendar included the Super Bowl, the Grammy Awards, the Daytona 500, and the Academy Awards.

Questions For Discussion

1. For what types of companies are the Olympics a particularly good advertising buy?

2. How does advertising on the Olympics differ from advertising on the Super Bowl?

3. Should Hollywood Studios attempt to become an exclusive sponsor of the Olympics? Why or why not?

4. If Hollywood Studios decides to bid on the Olympics, what price should they offer?

Glossary

Viral Marketing—word-of-mouth advertising via email passed among friends.

Product Placement—a fee paid by companies for their branded product(s) to be prominently displayed in a movie, TV show, or other media production.

Multivariate Regression Analysis—a form of statistical analysis that determines the strength of the relationship (correlation) between three or more independent variables.

Web Links

www.marketingpower.com, the web site for the American Marketing Association, providing marketing resources and links to various industry journals, including the *Journal of Marketing* and the *Journal of Marketing Research*.

www.nielsenmedia.com is the corporate web site for Nielsen Media Research, which conducts television audience measurement and related demographic services, and reports this information to advertisers, agencies, networks, and others.

www.ifilm.com/superbowl, the corporate website for IFILM, provides video clips of current and past Super Bowl television commercials.

www.comcastspotlight.com, the corporate website for marketing intelligence firm ComCast Spotlight, provides basic advertising media information including a glossary of terms, discussion of the various types of media and their suggested best use, and links to related sites.

5. Chinook Traders Thank-You Business

Product Positioning

Student Entrepreneurial Spirit[1]

Dr. John Claxton

How do you take a successful local businesses and move to a national and international scale? Everyone seems to think that the 2010 Olympics will provide an opportunity to do just that. Janet Harvey and Clara Arnold, the co-directors of the Chinook Traders Thank-you Business, have been told repeatedly that they are facing the opportunity of a life-time. Politicians and Aboriginal business leaders see the tourism associated with 2010 as a wonderful opportunity for local Aboriginal businesses to tap into new markets. But how do you take a little business initiated to help build Aboriginal business skills to the next level? Or would it would be better to follow the old dictum, "stick to your knitting"?

Early Days

The Chinook Traders initiative[2] was started to provide Aboriginal high school students with an opportunity to learn about **entrepreneurship** by participating in business activities. The co-directors, both Aboriginal women with business education and experience, started by evaluating other entrepreneurship programs.[3] This led to the idea of engaging a team of high school students in a summer workshop with follow-up team meetings via conference calls. The summer workshop provided an overview of the steps

---

[1] Copyright © 2005 Chinook Program, Sauder School of Business, University of British Columbia.

[2] Initial funding support for the Chinook initiative was provided by Terasen Inc. http://www.chinook.com.

[3] The National Foundation for Teaching Entrepreneurship was a helpful source: http://www.nfte.com.

involved in starting a new business (Appendix A). The Sunday evening conference calls, particularly in the early weeks, focused on identifying new business ideas. Dozens of products and services were considered, but none of the initial ideas seemed to provide the potential needed for success.

The Breakthrough

The products selected for the new business were foil-covered chocolate coins and cards. The breakthrough came when the business idea was seen not as selling candy and cards, but as selling *thank-you's* (or máhsie, in Chinook, the traditional language of trade. This business would not involve kids standing outside supermarkets selling candies one by one. Rather, the customers would be all the people and organizations that need a small gift to say thank-you to friends, employees or customers. The business would involve selling thank-you's by the box.

Start-up

With the business idea defined, the next step was to find suppliers for the needed products and packaging. Who could supply chocolate coins with the Chinook logo embossed? Who could supply high-quality greeting cards, and who could supply the

packages and printing needed? The criteria used to select suppliers were quality, cost, and business values that emphasized customer service. After evaluating a dozen firms, the team decided to use Charlie's Chocolate Factory, the Great Little Box Company, and Mountain Printing & Graphics Inc.

Left: A box full of *thank-you's*: 10 boxes of chocolates and 10 cards/envelopes
Top: Five boxes of foil-covered chocolate coins
Bottom: Ten cards and envelopes

In addition to providing good products and good prices, each of these suppliers welcomed the opportunity to help a group of high school students get a new business off the ground.

With products in hand it was time to find some customers. For a practice run the team headed for Vancouver's Granville Island Public Market. By the end of a day at the market, everyone on the team was comfortable talking to customers about the products and the Traders project, and it was clear that the business had potential.

As the thank-you business got rolling, it became clear that both corporations and Aboriginal organizations were enthusiastic customers. As hoped, these customers have many occasions when they want to say thank-you, and see it as a real convenience to have a supply of nicely packaged gifts. The packaging tells the story of the business and of the students' plan to use business proceeds to contribute to the annual Aboriginal Elders Conference. A nice gift. A nice sentiment. Happy customers.

The next challenge was to identify ways to communicate with customers, and to establish dependable means of processing orders and making deliveries. The high school students participating in the project are from various parts of British Columbia. This is both an advantage and a disadvantage. On the positive side, it provides a natural sales force spread around the province. On the other hand, managing transactions and inventories needs extra care.

So What About 2010?

The 2010 Olympics seems to be an ideal opportunity for all local companies. In making their decision, the business managers will need to answer many questions. Starting with thinking about current customers, questions to consider include the following:

1. Make a list of the type of organizations that likely buy thank-you gifts. How do organizations such as these purchase thank-you gifts?

2. Who in the organization is likely to be involved in the purchase of thank-you gifts?

3. What sources might they use when purchasing thank-you gifts?

4. What communications could Chinook Traders use to get the attention of these customers?

5. What steps could be taken to make it easy for these customers to buy from Chinook Traders?

6. What price would you recommend for the box of thank-you's (10 boxes of chocolates and 10 cards)?

7. What costs and volumes would make this an interesting venture?

When considering how their understanding of the current customers would apply to customers resulting from 2010, the business managers will also need to consider the following:

8. Who would be the new customers that could be attracted because of 2010?

9. What communications could Chinook Traders use to get the attention of these new customers?

10. What steps could be taken to make it easy for these new customers to buy from Chinook Traders?

11. What is the estimated total cost of attracting these new customers?

12. Does this look like a promising opportunity for Chinook Traders?

Appendix A – Chinook New Business Planning Guide

1. VALUES

What **values** guide your business planning?

What **vision** & goals do you hope to achieve?

2. IDEAS

What is your business idea?

What product/service will you offer?

What price will customers pay?

Where will customers buy it?

What will you name your business?

How will you be better than competitors?

3. CUSTOMERS

Who will your customers be?

What do they look for in your type of product/service?

Where do they currently buy your type of product/service?

How many customers are there in the area you will serve?

How many of these customers do you hope to attract?

How do you intend to attract these customers?

What market research do you have about customers?

4. PROFITS

How much money will you make on each unit sold?

Selling price per unit?

Variable costs per unit?

Contribution margin per unit?

What will be your day-to-day expenses that are not included in your variable costs?

What will be your one-time expenses to get started?

5. RESOURCES

MONEY: One-time expenses to get started? (equipment, deposits, inventory, salaries)

SKILLS: Special skills needed? (What skills are needed? Who will provide these skills?)

ENERGY: People available to day-to-day work? (What day-to-day work? Who will do it?)

6. STEPS - PROJECT PLANNING

Steps to get the business running?

What major steps are needed?

What deadline to complete each step?

Who is responsible for each?

Questions For Discussion:

1. How important is mentorship in achieving success for new entrepreneurs?

2. How important is the quality of the chocolate to the success of the venture?

3. Does a business or the consumer decide a product's category?

4. How do consumers differentiate between products in a product category?

Glossary

Entrepreneurship—talent for recognizing business opportunities and the abilities to develop them into profit-making companies.

Values—the guiding principles and beliefs a firm demonstrates in achieving its business goals.

Vision—an idealistic description of what success for the firm would look like.

Web Links

www.sbinfocanada.about.com, sponsored by the Government of Canada, provides a variety of resources to new business and entrepreneurs.

www.canadaone.com, the website for *Canada One Magazine*, provides resources for small businesses. Federal and Provincial government resources are made available to young entrepreneurs at **www.canadaone.com/magazine/loan_programs.htm**.

www.cbsc.org, sponsored by the Government of Canada, provides links to the various government programs, services, and financial assistance available to young entrepreneurs.

www.yea.ca, the website for the Young Entrepreneurs Association of Canada, provides peer mentorship opportunities and resources to young entrepreneurs.

6. Alpha Aviation Inc.

New Product Development

We must build it, they are coming.

Cindy Stewart

Boundary Bay Airport was first developed as a flight training centre for Air Force pilots during World War II. Today, Boundary Bay Airport (BBA) is the fifth busiest airport in Canada[1], with approximately 200 000 take-offs and landings per year. Much of this activity results from being home to six flying schools and a major flying club with a membership of more than 1000 local flying enthusiasts. Even so, its new owner, Alpha Aviation Corporation, and many others consider BBA to be an underutilized resource.

Only 9 acres of the 168-acre site have been developed for aviation-related industry. Located on-site are three privately owned hangar buildings, one terminal building, one flight centre offering office and hangar space for business applications, and the heritage World War II hangar. Also found on site is a full-service air traffic control tower supported by NavCanada, staffed from 7 am to 11:30 pm seven days a week. One half of the World War II hangar is used for aircraft hangarage, and the other half houses aircraft maintenance. Both the heritage hangar and flight centre properties are operated by the Pacific Flying Club under a **land lease agreement**. At the privately owned hangar buildings there are approximately 40 hangar bays offered to own or rent.

---

[1] Alpha Aviation: www.czbb.com, accessed on June 10, 2005.

Emerging Opportunities

Alpha Aviation believes there is great potential for the airport to grow its revenue base from corporate jet and region carrier customers. Current revenue sources include fuel sales, land and building space rentals, landing fees, and parking fees for aircraft and vehicles. Transportation Canada recently reactivated BBA as a general aviation airport to mitigate any potential safety hazard to heavy commercial jets[2] from the air traffic congestion created by the increased light aircraft now stationed at Vancouver International Airport (YVR). Transport Canada would like to relocate these aircraft to BBA. Furthermore, the resulting capacity problems from increased air traffic at YVR are expected to worsen in the coming years; creating an opportunity to relieve a portion of this general aviation traffic from YVR to BBA. Other revenue expansion opportunities also exist. Private hangar developers are keen to increase the existing capacity and a heli-operator has expressed interest in building facilities at BBA.

Private and corporate jet ownership is on the rise. With the introduction of **fractionalized ownership**, corporate jet ownership has become an economical alternative to business class travel on commercial airlines[3]. From 2001 to 2002 fractionalized private jet ownership grew 500% and business jet flights rose 13% in the United States alone.[4] This trend is expected to grow exponentially with the introduction of jet cards[5] and private plane ownership in China[6]. However, most corporate jets cannot fly across the Pacific, so little increase in international flights from corporate China is expected in Vancouver.

---

[2] Alpha Aviation:www.czbb.com/history.shtml accessed on June 10, 2005.

[3] According to Kevin Russell, Chief Executive Officer of the Berkshire Hathaway–owned NetJets, outright ownership only makes sense for businesses that require at least 500 hours of flying time or 62 working days in the sky per year.

[4] Joe Sharkey, "Security Is Looser On Corporate Aircraft," *The New York Times,* Late Edition, October 28, 2003.

[5] At Marquis Jet, companies buy only flight time in increments of as little as 25 hours for a fee ranging from US$110 000 to US$340 000 or US$4400 per flight hour, depending on aircraft. Sales of their jet cards rose 200% from 2002 to 2003.

[6] Until January of 2004, private jet ownership was not formally allowed in China.

Often-cited benefits of private jet ownership include increased speed, security, privacy, and efficiency; it's a 1000 kph boardroom. The majority of corporate aircraft operate from private terminals at domestic airports that do not handle commercial air traffic[7]. Private terminal usage provides increased security to high-profile fliers. Their car can pull straight up to the aircraft. Efficiency is also improved by avoiding the commercial flight check-in line-ups and by being able to fly into a nearby airfield rather than having to drive from the closest hub airport.

When the 2010 Olympic Games are held in Vancouver the Organizing Committee (Vanoc) would like to see the 500 corporate jets expected to arrive each day handled at a dedicated business terminal. Minimum ancillary services required at the terminal would include customs and immigration, passenger and crew lounges, and office space. Vanoc would also like to see on-site retail, land transportation, and food services. Developing a dedicated terminal is expensive. At this time Vanoc has not provided for constructing one in its megaproject construction program[8].

Meeting Expectations

To learn more about the service and facility demands of Olympic corporate jet traffic, Alpha board members visited Salt Lake City. From their visit they learned that a dedicated maintenance hangar and increase hangar capacity would have to be constructed along with the ancillary

Aerial view of the Boundary Bay Airport lands

services required by Vanoc. Currently BBA offers tarmac and grass parking for 300 airplanes and about 20 hangars for rent. The cost to build an airport hangar is estimated to be $1 million dollars per row. A typical row parks between six and eight airplanes. According to Mark

[7] Sharkey, *The New York Times,* October 28, 2003.
[8] "Building the Dream," *Vancouver Sun,* 12 February 2005, C3.

Cunningham of Riley Aviation, individual hangars would have a market value of about $250 000. The construction cost for a maintenance hangar is estimated to be $4 million.

Before Alpha starts courting new business partners, many improvements to the aging infrastructure on the field must be completed: resurfacing the apron, providing for greater safety overrun capability on one runway, installing a precision approach path indicator (PAPI), and overlaying the end of runway 25. New security measures are also required. These include installating electronically controlled gating, perimeter fencing, and a security pass system. The total cost of these upgrades is estimated to be $6.5 million dollars, of which Alpha and the Corporation of Delta plan to contribute $1.2 million. Federal and provincial government grants are being sought to fund the balance.

Competing Interests

Not everyone agrees that BBA is the ideal choice for relocating YVR light aircraft or that it should be the primary host of corporate jets visiting the Olympic Games. Some suggest Abbotsford Airport because of its full-sized runway and excess capacity. Environmentalists are concerned about further expansion of BBA because it is situated in the Pacific flyway, a migration route for birds heading to South America from Alaska. However, visitors would likely prefer BBA because it is closer: just thirty minutes south of Vancouver city centre, whereas Abbotsford is at least a one-hour drive—when it's not rush hour.

Questions For Discussion

1. Which airport do you feel is the best choice to relocate light aircraft to?

2. Do you agree that it is necessary to develop a dedicated business terminal for the Olympics?

3. What types of on-site retail and food services should be provided to business jet Olympic visitors?

Glossary

Land Lease Agreement—a rental agreement for a specific parcel of land that does not include capital improvements to be made by the landlord. At the end of the lease, any improvements to the property made by the renter must be removed or their ownership reverts to the landlord.

Fractionalized Ownership—an arrangement whereby ownership of an asset is shared among many people based on an agreed formula such as total number of days, total number of hours, or total square metres. An individual owner's entitlement is his/her prorata portion of the total invested capital.

Web Links

www.czbb.com is a website operated by Alpha Aviation Corporation providing general information about Boundary Bay Airport.

www.atac.ca is the website for the Air Transport Association of Canada (ATAC), an association of industry professionals that provides regional and national information about the aviation industry.

www.tc.gc.ca is the website for Transport Canada, where you can learn more about its role regulating commercial airlines, security, and the transportation of dangerous goods.

www.pacificflying.com is the website for the Pacific Flying Club.

www.navcanada.ca is the web site for NavCanada, an air navigation service that provides air traffic control, flight information, weather briefings, airport advisory services, and electronic aids to navigation.

7. *Vancouver Convention & Exhibition Centre*

Expanding Into New Market Segments

Leveraging your reputation for success

Cindy Stewart

History of Existing Site

Although it seems as though the renowned five-sails roofline has graced the city of Vancouver's skyline of forever, it was less than 20 years ago that the

Internationally recognized roofline of
Vancouver's convention centre

landmark waterfront Vancouver Convention & Exhibition Centre (VCEC) began hosting some 350 world events and 650 000 daily delegates each year[1]. Since its beginning as the Canada Pavilion during Expo '86, convention and trade show activities have generated benefits totalling about $250 million each year to all regions and sectors in the province.[2] In addition to its 40 full-time staff, the VCEC relies on seven official and contracted suppliers to provide a pool of more than 1400 part-time staff delivering the top-tier customer service Vancouver has become famous for.

The existing facility was designed to meet the needs of conventions ranging in size from 1000 to 2500 peak-night delegates. Within eight years of its opening, dramatic changes in demand for large conventions (2500+ peak-

---

[1]"About Vancouver Convention and Exhibition Centre," available from www.vanconex.com/corporate/index.html, viewed May 28, 2005.

[2] Vancouver Convention Centre Expansion Task Force, *Expanding the Vancouver Convention and Exhibition Centre Business Plan,* October 2000, p. 7.

night delegates) created a lucrative opportunity for revenue expansion, but the existing facility was unable to meet the unique facility design requirements of

this **market segment**. A pioneering P3 partnership among the provincial government, the City of Vancouver, and private-sector developer Greystone Properties Ltd. hatched the Portside Development proposal in 1995. The proposal called for a new convention facility with a clear span hall of 200 000 square feet, a thousand-room hotel, and an additional cruise ship berth.[3]

According to the plan, the developer would own the structure; the provincial government would finance the project and enter a lease-back arrangement between the developer and BC PAVCO, the convention management crown corporation. Navigating all the competing **stakeholders**' interests proved to be a monumental undertaking and ultimately led to the collapse of this initiative in 1999.

Expanding VCEC's Calendar of Events

Meanwhile, others have also recognized the economic windfall to communities hosting convention events,[4] and competition from other Canadian, U.S., and international cities for event bookings is fierce. *Tradeshow Week* recently reported that there are 377 exhibition and convention facilities in North America offering 65.2 million square feet of space. Canada has 40 facilities (10.6% of the market) providing 7.7 million square feet of space (11.8%). In North America there are currently 87 new and expanded facilities planned or under construction that will offer a total of 14.2 million square feet of new exhibit space and 3.3 million square feet of meeting space.

The convention and exhibit business comprises six distinct types of event: conventions, international congresses, corporate meetings, incentive shows, trade shows, and consumer events.[5] The most common themes are medical/science, technology, business/financial, and emerging industry. Events vary in demand for peak-night guest rooms, technological capability, on-site configuration flexibility, and ancillary site services such as ballrooms,

---

[3] "Clark Admits BC Tab Growing," *Daily Commercial News and Construction Record,* July 8, 1999, p. A1.

[4] Consumer events generate the least amount of economic activity, as 90% of attendees reside in the local community.

[5] *Expanding the Vancouver Convention and Exhibition Centre Business Plan,* pp. 42-43.

plenary rooms, and speciality services. Other important **customer preferences** include off-site services such as safe, interesting locations offering easy access and a diversity of cultural and recreational experiences.

Creating New Space

For lack of space or available dates, VCEC is currently turning away an average of 53 events per year, mostly large conventions, worth an estimated $150 million in direct delegate spending.[6] The current expansion task force regrouped in 2000 with a narrowed mandate of constructing a new convention complex only. Next it restructured the proposal to pursue funding from the federal and provincial governments, the major beneficiaries from convention revenue streams in the form of sales and business income taxes.[7] Ownership concerns raised in the initial proposal were dealt with too; the new facility would be owned by the provincial government. Finally, the current task force successfully lobbied both levels of government to contribute $650 million of the required capital investment by marrying the convention centre expansion to the core development plan for the 2010 Olympic Games.

The approved expansion project will more than triple the convention space to 1.2 million square feet, including both function and support spaces as well as parking, retail, and loading areas. An additional 359 000 square feet of function space will be added to the existing 133 000 square feet for a combined total of 492 000 square feet of meeting, exhibition, ballroom, and plenary space. The new site and design address the top priorities of event organization—building access, arrangement of spaces, adjacencies, traffic separation, loading efficiency, and flexibility of spaces[8]. Furthermore, the site design addresses the top infrastructure priorities of event efficiency and flexibility of space configurations. It also addresses a number of deficiencies in the existing facility, including limited access, inadequate loading facilities, and overlapping traffic flows[9].

There are three planned phases to the expansion project: constructing the new facility; upgrading the existing facility; and constructing an interconnecting

[6] "Expansion: FAQs" available from www.vanconex.com/expansion/faq.html, viewed May 28, 2005.
[7] *Expanding the Vancouver Convention and Exhibition Centre Business Plan,* p. 104.
[8] Ibid, p. 37.
[9] Ibid, p. 24.

walkway. The building budget for the total project is estimated at $565 million[10]. The construction budget for the new facility, to be completed by the summer of 2008, is estimated at $510 million. To make the two facilities aesthetically compatible, the existing convention centre will undergo a $15 million upgrade after the new building is complete. Finally, the two facilities will be physically joined together by two covered walkways costing $40 million.[11] All construction is to be completed by the fall of 2009.

Questions for Discussion

1. Who are the customers of VCEC?

2. What specific information do we need about the convention marketplace, and how does this information affect an expansion decision?

3. What impact will the new convention facility have on the profitability of the existing convention centre?

4. When the incremental sales and business taxes generated from new business ventures exceed the revenue expectations of private enterprises, should governments always fund the development of new mega projects?

Glossary

Market Segment—a group of consumers who respond in a similar way to a given set of marketing efforts.

Stakeholder—an individual or group having a vested interest in the activities undertaken by a company.

Customer preferences—the collection of product attributes that delivers the highest value to a consumer.

Web Links

www.vanconex.com is the corporate website for the Vancouver Trade and Convention Centre.

www.boardoftrade.com is the website for the Vancouver Board of Trade.

---

[10] Tourism BC will contribute $90 million; VCEC will contribute $30 million; and the federal and provincial governments will contribute $222.5 million each.

[11] John Les, "Convention Cente Gets A $40 Million Add-on," *The Province,* April 9, 2004, p. A.29.

The official business plan for the successful convention centre expansion project can be found at **www.boardoftrade.com/policy/reports/ConventionCentreBusPlan_oct2000.pdf.**

www.vccep.bc.ca is the website for the Vancouver Convention Centre Expansion Project.

8. Whistler Bike Park

Cross-Promotion Strategies

Extreme revenues year round

Cindy Stewart

A History of Fun

Who knew in February of 1966 that the ski village of Whistler, British Columbia, would grow up, along with its sister mountain Blackcomb, to become one of the most popular ski resorts in the world? But it hasn't always been a smooth ride. The original owners went bankrupt trying to operate the site as a ski resort only. When Intrawest Resorts Inc. created a business plan to purchase Whistler/Blackcomb Mountains (WBM) in 1986, it was quick to recognize that the success of the venture did not depend solely on the number of glaciers and the vertical drop. Skiers and boarders would always come for that. But to support the huge infrastructure investment required to create a world class resort, they would need to build revenue streams spanning four seasons.

Scenic bike trails for all abilities located at Whistler

The natural alpine beauty of the surrounding Garibaldi mountain community would attract short stay tourists in the summer, but there simply aren't enough of them. Repeat visitors drive the success for the snow season, and they would need to dominate the other seasons too. According to Intrawest, almost 70% of winter revenues result from repeat visits by Vancouver and Washington State residents. This customer base has two distinct **customer segments**: 1) affluent adults with children and 2) extreme sports enthusiasts.

Their choices in summertime recreation are worlds apart. Recognizing that one group currently dominated, Intrawest concentrated first on developing family and mature adult fun.

Watching the Radar

At the same time, Intrawest started tracking the summer activities of young extreme-winter-sports enthusiasts. They soon discovered a huge overlap in snowboarders and summer extreme-sport participation. Since the mid-80s, extreme bikers have been descending mountain peaks in Whistler. However, extreme biking has been slow to diffuse from the fringe to the mainstream. The world's first official extreme bike park opened at WBM in 1999. Today, it has become the world's biggest high-performance rental bike fleet, ready to challenge a rapidly expanding customer base with over 200 km of mountain trails punched with 1500-m vertical drops in 45 trails designed for beginner, intermediate, and expert thrill seekers. Jump farm trails and skills centres are also designed for different abilities.

Extreme terrain bike trails at Whistler Bike Park

As the extreme teens burgeoned into 50 million young adults with $450 million to spend,[1] Intrawest developed its **trend-spotting** techniques to identify other emerging extreme sports, such as trapezing, bungee trampolining, and all-terrain luging. All of these have been added to summertime fun at Whistler/Blackcomb. To spread the word to local snowboarders, Intrawest has drawn on its central reservation system to develop a marketing data bank of season's pass holders, edge card buyers, repeat visitors, and people who sign up for lessons or rent boards or skis.

Leveraging its **datamining** expertise, Intrawest has segmented its customers into discrete media groups. Young adults receive a monthly email newsletter

---

[1] "The U.S. Youth Market: Deciphering the Diverse Life Stages and Subcultures of 15 to 24 Year-olds", *Packaged Facts,* July, 2003, available at www.marketresearch.com.

highlighting upcoming boarding and biking events and what's new in extreme challenges. During April, May and June, cross-over promotions encourage boarders to ride and bike on the same day, using a combo lift ticket offered at a reduced price. **Activation events** such as Crud To Mud, Crankworx, and Harvest Huckfest have been developed to reinforce the social status of the sport. A select group of corporate sponsor partners including Contiki Tours, Trojan, Red Bull, Powerade, and Telus provide the additional resources needed to create weekends of world-class entertainment featuring bands such as Black Eyed Peas and Cheese String Incident.

Younger boarders are offered family rate packs and discounted accommodations in cross-over promotions for summer bike camps hosted by extreme biking icons. These offers piggyback on the youth and family season's-pass drive. Recent bike park improvements have included family-friendly trails and skills parks. Social connections to the sport are also developed for this group, but with more family-friendly **activation events** that showcase top-tier riders such as Richie Schley and Andrew Shandro in extreme competition events like the Mountain Slopes Style Event.

Changing Focus

The marketing strategies have paid off; bike park visitorship has grown 700%, from 10 000 rider days in 1999 to 78 000 in 2004,[2] split 75/25 between young adults and families. Achieving this year's ambitious goal of 90 000 rider days will be more difficult because the bike park's success has bred competition. Similar parks have recently opened or are slated to open throughout North America, both at other Intrawest resorts and at neighbouring ski resorts Sun Peaks and Mt. Washington. Due to the increased competition, Intrawest is exploring ways to raise the international profile of the sport to increase foreign visitor ride days to 20% of total revenues.

Until recently the international audience for bike parks hasn't been large enough to warrant a separate promotional investment. Foreign visitor awareness for the bike park has been generated mostly by billboards on the main highway into town, resort brochures, and the local television station, Resort TV. Past industry partnerships have been limited to informal relationships with international riders for trail development and bike event

---

[2] "Early Opening Shatters Records," available at www.whistlerblackcomb.com.

planning. Bike manufacturer partnerships have focused on website cross-promotion and local event sponsorship activities.

To capitalize on the world-wide attention for the Whistler/Vancouver Games in 2010, Intrawest's marketing plans for the bike park will focus on the four-seasons resort story. Expanded promotion efforts will include ad buys and feature stories in snowboarding and mountain biking magazines at crossover time; tour packages for the rapidly expanding specialty tour operators offering extreme sport adventures; and continued development of the international competition circuit. Furthermore, many Olympic-themed activation events are now on the drawing board; some focus on generating pre-Game publicity while others will be held during the Games.

Intrawest owns and operates many other resorts throughout North America. They include other ski resorts, Canadian Mountain Holidays heli-skiing operation, Abercrombie & Kent luxury/adventure travel, Club Intrawest, and Sandestine Golf resorts. Intrawest is also developing a European resort division. While no specific cross-promotion strategies are currently in place, they are being developed to raise awareness for Whistler's 2010 Olympic Games and its four seasons of fun, including the bike park.

Questions For Discussion

1. Will marketing the same product to both families and young adults adversely affect the brand's image for either customer segment?

2. How critical is a product's social status to its evolution from fringe to mainstream?

3. What makes Whistler's bike park unique?

4. Should cross-promotion strategies be developed for all the other resorts owned by Intrawest, or are some better choices than others?

Glossary

Customer Segments—discrete subgroups of the target market, found to be unique in their shared needs and values and expected response to a product, that command enough purchasing power to be of strategic importance to a company; identified using demographic, psychographic, and behaviouristic profiling.

Trend-spotting—identifying the general direction popular taste is currently moving.

Datamining—the analytical process of finding new and potentially useful knowledge from data.

Activation Events—events or series of events used to carry out a promotional strategy.

Web Sites

www.whistlerblackcomb.com is the corporate web site providing information for all recreation facilities owned and operated by Intrawest in the Blackcomb/Whistler area.

www.nsmbfc.com is the website for the North Shore Mountain Bike Festival and Conference, held in North Vancouver and Whistler during the last week of May and first week of June this year.

Credits

Case 1
pp. 2 and 4, Courtesy Olympia Pizza.

Case 2
pp. 8 and 9, Copyright © 2005 McDonald's Corporation and its affiliates.

Case 5
p. 30, Copyright © 2005 Chinook Traders.

Case 6
pp. 35 and 37, Courtesy Alpha Aviation Corporation; p. 37, Photo taken by Brad Pryde.

Case 7
p. 41, Courtesy Canada Place Corporation.

Case 8
pp. 47 and 48, Courtesy Intrawest Inc.